Bird Dog Publishing

Shepherds Among Us

A Poetic Memoir

Trenda Geller

Harmony Series
Bird Dog Publishing
Huron, Ohio

Credits
Editor & Design: Lary Smith
Cover Art: Martha Wikel
Cover Design: Susanna Sharp Schwacke

Acknowledgments

I would like to give a special thanks to the following:

Jim Geller – My loving husband and in-home cheerleader.

Pat Eckelberry – My oldest supportive sister for her technical
  support.

Tiffany Branco – A friend who has also been there for
  technical support.

Larry Smith – A true shepherd of creative voices.

Emily Dickinson – A model who has been there all along.

TABLE OF CONTENTS

I.   HEAVENLY

11. Loved Lamb
12. Garden of Eden
13. Ode To Grammy I
14. Ode To Grammy II
15. Ode To Grammy III
16. Grieving Grammy
17. Dad's Idea
18. Family
19. Manifestation of Intention

II.   HURTING

23. Scars
24. Premenstrual Madness
25. Her Way Out
26. Getting Out of Bed
27. Girlfriend Don't Go
28. Vision Quest
29. Somewhere Else
30. Essence of Floating
31. Dark Nights
33. The Reading
34. Prelude to Fall
35. Last Visit
36. Defeated
37. Just Say It
39. Hope Is an Extended Finger
40. Wayward Wanderer
41. Blonde & Blue-Eyed
42. Grief
43. War Revisited
44. The Shepherd
45. Honey Locust Stump
46. The Acid Taste Test

47. White-Collared Reputation
48. The Light Behind the Door
49. Emily And the Priest
50. Shepherds Among Us
51. Mother

III.   HELPING

55.   Rookie Social Worker
56.   The Elder
57.   Break Free
58.   Art of Counseling
60.   Oz On the Job
62.   Flying And Crying
63.   Bipolar Love
65.   Let the People Lie
66.   12 Lambs Leaping
67.   Finding Their Way
68.   Healing Properties
69.   Dance Club Blues
70.   Life In Threes
71.   Handful Of Insomnia
72.   Termination
74.   Carrer Challenge
76.   After Working 8-5
77.   Blowing Words
78.   Babe With Wings
80.   Chiseling the Mirage
82.   One's Life Is a Message

IV.   HEALING

85.   Covid No. 3
86.   Dear Karma
87.   Nostalgia
88.   Home
89.   Fathers Are Good Audiences
90.   Fishermen

91. From Bed to Moon
92. Sister
93. No Thank You
94. Namaste
95. Idle Hands Clapping
96. Jim Day
97. Still Unknown
98. Retrospect
99. Sunday Morning
100. Driving Mr. Daisy
101. Grace
102. Still Waters
103. Sanctuary
104. Surrender

106. Author Profile

I. Heavenly

A happy family is but an earlier heaven.
—George Bernard Shaw

LOVED LAMB

"The Lord is my shepherd,
I shall not want."
                    - Psalms 23:1

I grew up on a farm with my dad, grammy and grandpa
with fields, an orchard, creek, trees, animals and a wide
open sky above me—
            and something inside me bigger
            than all of it.

As a child I wandered the lanes between the crops,
watched the cows in the pastures, the butterflies, squirrels,
collected eggs in the chicken coop—
            explored nature until I felt
            one with it.

Grammy disciplined me gently, Dad more harshly,
especially when I threw kittens into the outhouse
and cistern. Dad taught me which weeds to pull out
of the garden and rhubarb patch.
            Grandpa let me ride
            with him on the tractor.

Sunday school and church were weekly—sick or not.
Grammy tucked me in bed every night and taught me
prayers and scripture—especially the 23rd Psalm.
            The farm had many animals.
            I was the only lamb.

GARDEN OF EDEN

Every time I hear
a mourning dove
you are in its song—

your pale wrinkled hand
with age spots, holding mine,
serenaded by the squeaks
of the vinyl porch glider.

The kittens scamper in the yard.
Butterflies hover near
blue morning glories,
as bees buzz closer to the pollen.

A squirrel runs up,
then back down
an old oak tree.
A cow moos, the dog barks.

Summer days with you
on the farm have lasted
all the seasons of my life.

ODE TO GRAMMY I

I remember the day we both
had to say goodbye
to the farm.
You cried and inside I swelled
with rivers and small streams
of nostalgia.

From a newborn you had raised me there.
You nurtured me with the inner
nature of the earth.
As I grew older you would wait up
half the night and worry
I was in such a hurry
to go astray.

You taught me how to bake, sew, plant
a garden, hoe a field,
and when you died
I forgot.

Though barns have burned and meadows
have been replanted, the soil still sticks
to my feet.
I will not walk away.

ODE TO GRAMMY II

The night God gave you wings
you came to me.
In silence you awakened me
and shook me from my bed.

Running to all the windows
I hoped to catch some movement
in the night.
But the night was dark and still.

Yet, once again
you had raised me
and are the flower in my womb.
O Godmother, O earth woman,
'O night air in the sky!

ODE TO GRAMMY III

Why did I fall asleep with you
on my mind—
awaken with you
and dream of you in between?
Your face. My words:
"Grammy, you came back!"

Though I was not
the flower of your womb,
you raised me.
O earth woman, Bible reader,
picker of strawberries
and baker of rhubarb pies.

How long before I stop missing
the sugar of your baked goods,
the sweetness of your eyes.

Not sure if I'll ever forget
your life, but
I've imbodied it into mine.

GRIEVING GRAMMY

After 30 years, I'm still pregnant
with nostalgia and this big
nothingness without you
rubbing my eyes, hoping to glimpse
one strand of your gray hair
so soft in my fingers.

You are not dead
just because I can't see you.
My arms ache without
you to hug.

Only words are left to whisper
into the sky and the mouths
of angels, hoping the heart
of your soul hears
how much, and how long
I will love you.

DAD'S IDEA

"Think for yourself or others will think
for you without thinking of you."
- Henry Thoreau

Back then, even before Grammy left her body,
Dad had an idea: he needed a family.
I, of course, had to join them
and leave my family.
So, he got married and I cried.

New mom tried. She made me
a blue and white gingham dress,
just like hers, and we all went
to the zoo. She'd go to church
with Dad and me.

She'd make us mush for supper,
cream of mushroom soup for lunch for me.
If I didn't eat it, she'd heat it up for
the next two days until I did.

First grade came. I was scared.
New mom walked me to the bus
at the end of our long lane beside
the railroad tracks.

But I liked my teacher, Mrs. Ruth,
a kind shepherd who taught me
how to read and write.
Now I could put my feelings on paper!

And so I begin—by age nine—
to write my first poem!

FAMILY

New mom wanted a family too.
Maybe I wasn't enough.
By the age of nine, I had three
sibs. By 17, six. By 20, seven.

They were a blessing. I was no longer
alone. I loved having four sisters.
They were so cute—and pretty.
The boys were brats. Later—lifesavers.

I am proud of them all: engineer, electrician,
construction worker, U.S. mail carrier, school
cafeteria manager, ophthalmic technician, and
deputy sheriff.

Each became great parents, aunts and
uncles. We were raised to be productive,
responsible and to respect our parents
and elders.

We lived in a devout Christian home,
prayed before meals. Mom was always
home when we got back from school.
Dad worked two jobs in the summer—
construction and farming with Grandpa
in the evenings.

I had my big family at last and we all loved
each other. Dad was the iron worker who
worked with iron rods building bridges and
tall buildings. Mom was the shepherd
who kept all of us lambs safe in the pasture
of our home.

MANIFESTATION OF INTENTION

Now I lay me down to
sleepless—
Grammy taught me to pray
otherwise.

With blurry vision
heart on fire

decades to go
before I rest
knowing so many
tests before me.

Daydreaming of purpose
amongst all
the flat-footed.

Stars tugging at my head
Showing me the way
north.

Wings on my feet
waiting.

II. Hurting

You have to keep breaking your heart
until it opens.
— Rumi

SCARS

Not wanting to feel
the cruelty of it all,
I scampered through
the dewy splendor
of the grass and fell —
burying my face in its blades.

Later, feeling a misty rain,
I sat up
looked into the sunless sky
and willingly removed my head
from my shoulders.
I cradled it in my lap.

PREMENSTRUAL MADNESS

Once a month Hades turns
the world into a belly-
flop, my tongue into sucking
straws for pomegranate seeds,
Poseidon's blue rivers
into dishes of snow.

He hides my swami yogi
between the sixth and seventh
chakra where I'll never
melt, transforms my morning
meditation into a cobra swirl.

I'm spitting seeds of impatience.
Let me be Cronus and swallow stones.
Let me be a ribless Adam.

If I can't be a male Israelite
crossing over the red sea,
then let me howl, "Creator,
lift down a box of blood,
I need a *deus ex machina!*"

HER WAY OUT

"Suicide kills two people…"
- Arthur Miller

Death came after slipping
off her black silk stockings
and drinking her last glass of merlot

like a blanket
pulled to the chest
at bedtime

like an alarm clock
set for a new day

like a man
spilling his semen
on the way to a dream

GETTING OUT OF BED

Only when my body falls to the floor, like a blanket
kicked off the bed by an early riser, will I awaken.
Like a child with new dreams, I will call "Abba, Father."
Like a snake with new skin, I will slither with a new gait.

Sleep is not always restful or pleasant.
Eyes not always rubbed the right way form images
of dying things, things that take you to dances,
movies, plays then bingo games.
You begin to call the images your friends
and the places their amends to better things.

O bed of feather pillows and tinker toys,
I have played with young soldiers on your high posts,
I have walked the crevices of your old blankets of darkness
more days than a bear hibernates for a season.
Now I must step down, down to the floor,
down and out to the gray paved streets.

GIRLFRIEND, DON'T GO

"A journey is best measured in friends
rather than miles."
                                        - Tim Cahill

So, you found a man
to hold your head
in his hands, with lips
that play a harmonica
to the strings of your heart.

A man who sends you roses,
respects his mother,
fishes with his father,
and sells cars to those
who may not want them.

You light up like a prom girl
until I question you: "Does he know
you deserve the sun, stars, moon
and tropical breezes all
before breakfast—
before the cock crows and the owl
closes its eyes?

If only you could see what I see.
Tilt your head. Look up at the rainbow.
Girlfriend, try to remember the dark in
the storm clouds that comes before rain.

VISION QUEST

Honor the day you walk
down that long dark corridor
of your psyche, sit in the parlor,
watch the cock fight, leave
with all your feathers intact.

Next day you fly to the desert,
wear your favorite perfume,
dance around the campfire
with stones between your toes
wearing a long skirt of turquoise hues.

In the dark you use your eyes
to unravel what lies beneath
the ashes, you blink when it coils
around your neck, kisses
your sun scorched lips.

Lying in the sand you draw
your knees up to your chest,
shiver beside the embers,
then nibble the marrow within
your bones to sustain you.

SOMEWHERE ELSE

He closed his eyes
        as he went down on her.
She took a long fingernail
        picked food from her teeth,
still yearning for the half-drunk
        glass of wine serenading
her from another room, as it sat
        beside her half-empty plate.

He groaned to put her in
        the mood; she sighed
to indicate a presence
        lingering somewhere else.

Dessert used to be a special
        occasion with tiny
bites in between sweet talk,
        dreams of how it could be
better than what it was then and there,
        not here and now,
like this moment
        where she is wanting
intoxication over ecstasy.

ESSENCE OF FLOATING

> "'Become nothing. Love will turn
> you into everything."
> - Rumi

Tonight—no one,
only the space I have fallen into
without knowing how to swim
in air or water.

Tonight—no one
who does not love either
his wife or mother.
I cannot understand why
I can't swim or fly above them.

Then I will float to you—
not by an act of will
but of development—like seaweed
drifting toward shore.

I will embrace you—
by touching
and by being
on a calm sunny day.

Most of all,
I will become patient—
as you carry me
to that place
where you no longer are.

DARK NIGHTS

I have danced with the devil's minion
wearing ruby red lipstick,
crimson stilettos and black silk stockings,
head on his shoulder
swooning to the music
'til dizzy and distant

from my spouse,
my true love—
the center of my soul
from long ago
and far away.

But his fencing with my intellect,
use of poetry, prose, promises
awakened my senses
thrusting me further into
the core of my being

Yet I yearned for my vows—
to that still small voice,
the light, peace and presence—
deep in my heart.

"Where is my hound of heaven?"
I cried out; he who can leap way
down into the caverns of corruption
where it is cold, dark and void of prayer.

The minion heard me—
wooed me with chocolate, flowers,
soothed my body with cocoa butter
and whispered sweet lullabies
into my ears.

Then my shepherd's voice—
in that peaceful whisper.
And I remembered. I still remembered,
as he rocked me gently, taking me
so far inward, away
from the minion's gaze and grip.

THE READING

They came to hang halos but found my head
lop-sided and before their eyes, I transformed
from an angel with a message
to an oracle of bad tidings.
Yet, dry-mouthed and charismatic
I spoke in tongues of Sexton, Plath,
Rich and Wakowski—filled with words
of wonder and worldly woe, wanting
to leave on the word 'go', staying,
realizing it was easier to swallow words
than to deliver them, unwelcomed,
like an enlightened baby in a dark-aged world.
Then with my mannerly "Thank you"
and their undertones of "For what?" they gathered up
the nouns, verbs, adjectives and pronouns
which they had heaped into their laps,
brushed them to the floor and walked out.
I was glad it was winter, glad
it was cold and snowing, that I had not come
in sandals, for I was convinced
they had come to hang me.

PRELUDE TO FALL

"Divorce can cause emotional chaos."
- Dr. Bill Doherty

Somewhere a bird is falling
from its nest, a dog is barking,
a tree is feeling the clawing
of its own roots.

The end of summer on Juniper Drive
is like a noisy train station
when the 5:15 pulls in.

Three men died last week
known to us both.
I called it the result
of your superstitions.
You called it luck
you weren't one of them.

The smell of autumn is
crispy as our son's cereal
set out for breakfast
the night before.

It wouldn't have to be
this way if you were
still here.

But now, silhouetted on some
dark backdrop are birds falling
into cereal bowls and trees clawing
at trains and dogs rooting in the night
for a dead man before breakfast.

LAST VISIT

For Dan

How many times
have our paths crossed
and now slowly into
different directions
mapped for a lifetime
of sorrow.

Like gaps, a chasm
only getting wider.
Your house is cold,
your bed colder,
traces of Alaska
all over the place.

Your suitcase, the plans
from the pipeline
you just helped build,
two phone numbers
on your nightstand,
whose Mercedes in the back yard?

Traces of tears
on your bedspread—
It's not all I have to offer,
but all I'll leave behind.

DEFEATED

> "It's madness to hate all roses because
> you got scratched with one thorn."
> - Antoine de Saint-Exupery

My life is unraveling
like a spool of yarn
knocked over by a cat.

Lowly and stooped
it wouldn't take much
to retrieve it,

yet, it feels like combat.
To forgive or to forget
are draining options.

Meanwhile I keep
paying the piper who
plays music for some king.

And I can no longer sing
as I trip over tangled yarn
on my hands and knees.

JUST SAY IT

Good-byes can be too long—
others too short.
Not only is it all
in the timing, but
in the creation
of the introduction—
the beauty of the beginning
of the very end.

Why say "hello" if you don't
plan to write the last page?

Go back to the timing—
were you shopping with money
in your pocket,
lonely on a rainy day?
Did you go out dancing
feeling young, invincible?
Were you afraid of how to pay the rent?

Haven't you learned by now
you can't walk onto a stage
without tripping over the props.

Look behind the curtain.
Look toward the door
the patrons came through.

Why would they duck into
a dark building to see
someone they don't know
to sit beside someone they just met?

You know. Just say it.
Because we live to see, feel
say good-bye from the other side,
way at the very end.

HOPE IS AN EXTENDED FINGER

> "Every attempt at a door or window
> has been blocked; yet they keep
> giving him hope."
> - Phillip F. O'Connor

You were a window.
I wanted to sit on your ledge,
feel the warm sun
pour into my face.

Instead, I walked the perimeters
of a small room, feeling the cracks
in the walls, matching them with
the cracks in my skull, wondering
if I could climb out.

Sartre couldn't find an exit—
why should I?

From much trampling
the floorboards squeak,
the ceiling is chipped
with the prodding of eyes
trying to lift it.

Even the furniture is gone,
leaving only one posture:
an extended finger
drilling the glass.

WAYWARD WANDERERS

Where are the virgins who walk
close to the holy one?

I search the churches,
the land, sky and see more flags
waving than empty crosses standing.

Too many bosses, too many men
seeking their daily bread,
touch of a woman
and footholds for egos
larger than feet.

Give me a sparrow that knows
which direction to fly.
Show me the lambs still quivering
from the lion's roar.

Where are the students who know
in and up are the same?

Forget this game of survival
on a board covered with ashes.
Show me a spot where I can stop, stand
and fall to my knees.

BLONDE & BLUE-EYED

"Before you were conceived I wanted you
Before you were born I loved you
Before you were here an hour I would die for you
This is the miracle of love."

-Maureen Hawkins

You, my first born, came
so early. I was so young.

Your dad was not ready
to fight that war in Vietnam.

Our love was great, his parting sad.
My daughter, you were and are the joy we have.

You challenged my parenting, made me
grow. When you were a teen, I just didn't know

if I could survive the worries.
You were in such a hurry to grow up.

You've always been a sweet older sister
to your younger brother.

Later, a wonderful mom, excellent cook, wife,
and a good- humored, loving friend to many.

You, a beautiful woman, did not come soon enough,
I just thank God you are my daughter.

GRIEF

The goddess of time must know
what she's doing when she says,
"Say goodbye to him."

Tell me how to do that?
I have held him in the fold of my hand,
felt the softness of his feathers,
the flutter of new flight within his breast.

I wanted to nurture him, offer him
forever teats flooding over with fresh milk,
wanted to clutch him to my chest,
feed him more heartbeats.

I wanted to wipe away all the blood and scars
from his journeys around the world,
his horrible 26 months in the Peace Corp
in Mongolia where he *almost died.*

He traveled and lived in Colorado, California, Alaska,
Cambodia, Spain and Thailand. With his college degree,
from California State, he taught English
to Thai students and government officials.

He had finally found and married the love of his life
five months before you took him. This beautiful, sweet,
intelligent Thai woman who I love lives so far away.
My precious, only son—you were only 48.

But the goddess of time took your hand,
blew you away, like a candle in a drafty barn.
I, however, wasn't finished rocking your cradle
in my heart—forever bleeding.

WAR REVISITED

The road to Baghdad is
a muddy trench cut
in the midst of all
our soldiers.

The sky there is dark,
not blue, blinding sand
blocking the sun that could dry
tears soldiers dare not shed.

No one sleeps at the Palestine Hotel;
all stand vigilant, children watch
as tanks roll through
streets they used to play in.

Ears grow deaf from B52s, F14s,
the stark silence at Saddam Airport
where no one can fly out of
or courageously fly into.

Reporters are warriors, dying for the truth.
There are not enough shovels,
not enough hands, not enough ears
to hear meek voices utter:
"I am an American too."

Last night I told my grandson:
"Your great-grandfather was in the 82nd,
your grandfather in the 101st.
Be proud of them. Rest your weary
little head in my wobbly lap
and count the sheep ten miles back
from the slaughter."

THE SHEPHERD

For Gene

Our souls lept
at first, proximity
then our eyes.
I knew you before.
I'll know you again.

As a professor you taught me.
As a landlord you were my neighbor.
As a pastor you led me, fed me.
I was your sheep.

You kept me in safe pasture
near a beautiful lake.
I did not want to stray.
I would have stayed.

But you found a shepherdess.
I got confused and wandered.
The thistles in the woods
pricked my skin everywhere.

I encountered black sheep
who taught me what
it looks like if they don't
listen to the shepherd.

With the help of other
unknown shepherds, I grew,
became the best version of me.
Looking back, I saw, I knew.

You were teaching me to be
a shepherd just like you.

HONEY LOCUST STUMP

"What can I give him,
Poor as I am?
If I were a shepherd
I would bring him a lamb.
If I were a wise man
I'd do my part.
Yet what can I give him?
I give him my heart."
                    - Christina Rosseti

There was a honey locust stump
in Lake Front Park.
You used to sit near enough
I could see the light
filtering through the foliage
of an oak on the other side.

At night the shadows would play
hide-n-seek around the steeple
across the street, and you,
my priestly shepherd, were tucked
snuggly away in bed down the block.

Unlike me, the honey locust stump
always seemed to survive your slumber.

THE ACID TASTE TEST

> "Truth does not change according to our
> ability to stomach it."
>
> - Flannery O'Connor

You damaged my teeth when you went off
to New York.
I had to bite down when she joined you.

Who a person sleeps with is no one else's
business.
And monthly dentist bills are simply an
evolutionary curse.

Have you ever sat in a dental chair and chanted
Chaucer under your breath while a white-coated
drill sergeant hummed his "Ode to Flossing"?

No? But you've lain in plush bridal suites
licking your sugar and thumbing your way through
some dark tunnel, and if I were there and had enough
teeth I'd bite you.

WHITE-COLLARED REPUTATION

Marriage—
was his holy sacrament
against any feelings of guilt.
So he took her.
Clothed in white,
he took her.
Veiled in net,
he took her.
Like a blue-eyed mermaid
he dreamt he was
a fisherman,
so he took her.
Fair-skinned, blond haired,
blushing cheeks, rosy lips,
he took her.
Because his first wife
left him for another
he took her.
Instead of a thief
in the night, he was
a fisherman, looking
for a sacramental vow—
Marriage.

THE LIGHT BEHIND THE DOOR

When you looked at me, you saw the sky,
stars, moon, clouds and sea. Yet, I thought
it was me who put the twinkle in your eyes,
me you loved, that small invisible seed that
believed it was a universe to itself.

I now kknow you spoke to a being within me,
someone or something higher, deeper than myself,
a being that hugs or lips could never reach.

The night you came to me without clothes or form
your bright light beckoned me to follow,
but the small pea of me just lay in bed dreaming
of water in a glass house, my nose to the window
pane watching you walk past.

I had a ticket to ride, but my fear hid in
the embryo of someone's lost womb and
I have been swimming upstream ever since.

Stop the waves and tides of the moon.
Spoon me into your invisible lap, like
a precious seashell you once stooped
to hear Lake Erie within. Put me to your ear—
hear the small beat of a heart that has

beaten all these years just to stand in
your presence, merged into only you.

EMILY AND THE PRIEST

Day is overcast—
joy undercast.
Emily understands
Amherst is the beginning
and the end.

Some feelings stay
like clouds and rain:
a cold damp pervades
through decades—
even longer.

Aye is the opposite of nay.
"Hey" you used to say,
and I would turn
just in time to see
the sun shine.

'Sunny' was the name
of your dog.
You had four boys, a wife
and your own church
where you went to pray.

Only you stayed.
She left and I was in
an extended season
with longing.

Now—look at us now
planted on three
different planets
overcast with rain.

SHEPHERDS AMONG US

Reluctantly moved from Huron,
hurting from the divorce,
from the shepherd
taking a shepherdess,
BGSU only having
associate degrees.

Moved to Bowling Green
pursuing the dream of becoming
a psychotherapist—to help people.
Then a master's degree from UM.

Steep path upon a winding road—
raising children, working full-time,
classes part-time.

If it hadn't been for shepherds
(Grammy, the pastor, professors)
I might have wandered
off the path.

Every step I took the shepherd
of the shepherds held my hand,
cleared rocks from the pasture
so I wouldn't fall below my knees.

Eventually I knew the dream
was a mission all along.
And maybe not just mine.

Hindsight
revealed this to me:
There are shepherds among us.

MOTHER

You gave up on me
to pursue you—
your slow downward spiral
of self-destruction.
I was seven months old.

Since then I have tried
to save you over
and over in thousands
of strangers, known
as clients and patients.

I'm a dry drunk obsessively chasing
the shadow of a full bottle
of your favorite vodka,
day in and day out
through darkness and light.

My sight grows dim from squinting
to overlook all the flaws
in our social work laws,
which initially teach us what
to do when assessing others.

The years have brought me into
and through the anxious, depressed,
and moody heads swimming
in some flavor of booze.
I cannot slumber—there are so many.

Mother, like a hound from hell,
since I suspect you've left your body,
you stalk my home, beheaded

both my children, poisoned
their bellies with your brew.

You—who they called
my "mother"—now beyond
me and all the training
that tells me birth cannot keep
birthing death.

Yet, I keep chasing for a cure
for you and the children, who
(Are they sober?)
keep drinking before my squinted eyes
breaking my heart.

But I will never stop trying
to help those who need care,
work on forgiving you
and keep healing me.

III. HELPING

The sheep in the pasture, the pasture,
Which is mostly rejoicing, since all the
ingredients are here...
— Mary Oliver

ROOKIE SOCIAL WORKER

There is a giant
in my bones
who believes it can
jump tall and wide
buildings, save people
from gunpoint, deliver
wine and wafers.

> There is a hero
> in my blood
> bleeding out fortitude,
> gushing with the myth
> it can protect
> prisoners from their own
> life circumstances.

> > There is half an ounce
> > of fear shivering in
> > my tears, in the middle
> > of the night, wondering
> > if even giants
> > and heroes are
> > bloated with wind.

THE ELDER

She came to me
face down,
lines drawn with wisdom,
old tears held inside
with emotions not yet
ready to share.

She had a life full
of accomplishments,
a humble shepherd
without a staff to lean on.
Sadness was penetrating
her heart and mind.

She was struggling with aging,
pre-grief of her spouse dying first,
feelings of worthlessness.
Anxiety and depression clouded
her mind with a daily
dreaded forecast.

She listened attentively, did
her homework, shared
her life. I painted for her her legacy.
She achieved beyond her treatment goals.
I gleamed when I heard
the crescendo of her smile.

BREAK FREE

So, when are you
going to find a place
of your own?

A roof covering four walls——
a room you do not share
with your parents, spouse,
lover, roommate, fiancé,
significant other or any other
member of a commune or
church culture that offers you
feather pillows or soft cushioned
benches with no moths.

When are you going to look
at an empty wall, pound
a nail into it, hang one
thing on it that speeds up
your own heart?

Birds can live on a wire,
a branch, a waft of air
going nowhere.

But you, my sad lamb,
keep searching for someone
else's womb to crawl into.

Break free, free from
the false drama
your fearful ego has created
to keep you from the man within,
the boy you have adopted.

ART OF COUNSELING

"Walk out of your house like a shepherd."
- Rumi

There are lepers among us
with invisible scars.
Is there an island in your mind
where you've banished them?

I've visited my island,
set up an office there,
watch people walk in,
smiles on their long faces.

They talk about abuse, rape,
abandonment, car crashes,
death of their children, loss
of jobs, or the holocaust.

There is no place in my being
I can or want to
banish them to.
So, I've taken up an art.

It takes special brushes
to dry the tears,
cleanse the scars,
wipe away the blood.

When they leave I
only hope their nightmares
subside a little,
that they sleep a couple hours more.

I keep hoping they come back
so we can work together
to slay the monsters that keep
terrifying their minds.

OZ ON THE JOB

Face distorted, he sat in
a chair across from me, calmly
stating. "The monkeys are back..."
I shifted, settled in,
bracing myself for a long session.

His voice held fear
as he described the clowns
in his childhood; the dark;
the sound of his father's death;
the empty toy room; supper on
the closet floor as he listened
to rats scurry in the walls.

I tell him he's safe now.
"Today is a new start;
let's create a good day..."
He looks through me as if to see
shadows dancing on the back wall.
He mumbles something to someone
I cannot see.

I ask him about his ADL'S, his meds,
his food intake, hygiene,
his pet bird. He tells me
the monkeys ate his bird
and now he is not hungry—
The medicine makes it too quiet
to talk to his friends.

I lean forward, trying to find
his eyes; I see clouds, shades
of another world I cannot visit.

I tell him I'm sorry about his bird,
he needs to take his meds.

Because quiet time with friends
is better than flying monkeys
in his home. I lightly click my heels
twice and remind us both—
"There is no place like home."

FLYING AND CRYING

They go so high
    dip so low.
I watch my bipolar patients
    with empathy,
    educatating,
    listening,
    listening some more.
This diagnosis became my specialty
    after a friend posted a note
    on her bedroom door
    to her sons, saying:
    "I'm napping."—
    then shot herself in the head
    for her husband to find.
The call came three days prior to my wedding.
    Pain and anger prompted me to study
    all the literature
    sharpen my professional skills.
But it was too late,
    for her
    for me.
Three months after marriage,
    I discovered my spouse had the same
    diagnosis—bipolar disorder—
    the most challenging of the four types.
My career and my marriage.
I listen and pray.
This is my curse and my blessing.
These are my sheep.

BIPOLAR LOVE

You touch my skin,
I bond like a baby
abandoned by a mother
at birth.

Now, in mid-life, I crave
the daily meal of your fingers
caressing my flesh—
that sweet succor
that says, "Yes, you are

soft enough to touch,
good enough to love,
fragile enough to nurture,
hungry enough to feed."

Yet, despite the delight
you are still suspect
to my latent bonding—
not my mother, but a man—

a man who needs
grown up love, not
a little girl lacking lust
who bruises with a wet tongue.

I am woman enough
not to run when your words
sting my flesh from the inside out
like a cold sharp knife
stabbing melting butter.

Touch me softly
or slap me boldly,
but don't sling words
that push me way back
into my mother's womb.

LET THE PEOPLE LIE

Let the people lie in your face,
they're scared but still need integrity.
There is too much on their plate
to digest in five minutes,
too little time to clean the windows
in their slave houses, then travel inside
and clean their rooms.

There has always been more work
than people in the fields to do it.

Muscles ache from the backpacks and luggage.
People are like mules with heads like bulls,
brains like birds, trying to board planes filled
with fear—and sometimes terrorists.
Their fantasized pinions are caught beneath
layers of earth-born rock.

Let the people lie in your face.
Some days it is the only tool they have.

12 LAMBS LEAPING

It's December—again.
They're crawling, leaping out
of my office walls
crying out—"Help me!"

The moody ones.
The ones whose prefrontal cortex's
have sent out a change
of guards.

Change is hard for them.
Especially holidays like this one.
They ask: "Will it be all I expect it to be?"
"Will I be good enough?", "Loved enough?"

Too much stimuli for them.
No routine. They ask: "Where
is the angel for the top of the tree?"
"If I'm not it, who can it be?"

Come Emmanuel—give me the words
through a trumpet so I can
tell them their curse is a gift.
Help me find the bow.

FINDING THEIR WAY

To assess without
judging
to know I am
no better
ever.

Asking St Anthony
of Padua
to find me
the thoughts and
words
to plant the seeds
they need to find
the way
that day
and back
to a path of well-
being and peace
within.

HEALING PROPERTIES

They say prayer is
listening
to the silence.
I've listened to
talking
confessing
crying
yelling.
For years my ears
have been bombarded
with sounds. I crave
silence.

In the listening
I learned to love
lepers
long-haired freaks
all those misunderstood.

My heart expanded
outside my body.

Now I pray
that I may
never be deaf
to the broken-hearted.

DANCE CLUB BLUES

Honey child, don't you know
you take your life way too seriously.
Relax, let the happenings slide off
your shoulders; let your arms
embrace the actions of others
as if you are the witness
they have not yet met.
Hug them with your eyes
in a moment's glimpse.
Kiss the clouds that await them
outside the door. Carry them
in your prayerful thoughts
to the march of drums
pounding in the streets.
Include them in your will
as numberless beings, worthy
of your whole life's work.
Baptize them with your first
born child; carry them
to the altar of your disgrace.
Confirm them with some holy blood.
Treat them as the Almighty
who just might ask you to dance.

LIFE IN THREES

One of my friends is a churchgoer who carries a pink girly gun.
Another lives in the desert; spends half her time with her grandkids
the rest drinking wine and planning trips to Baja.
I buy silk for my third friend, so sophisticated she turns
       everyone's head.
Three days a week I counsel those I cannot befriend, who
tell tales of great suffering: abuse, neglect, trauma, anxiety, depression,
relationships more toxic than children eating lead chips of paint
       off windowsills.

I talk to people so lonely, with no hope, no families, no friends.
They carry 9mm, chug bottles of booze and have no silk
pillowcases to lay their heads upon.

At night I calm my nerves with no wine, knock on the door of
       my higher self,
walk into my bedroom and lay my head on my cotton pillowcase
beside a nightstand with no gun. I pull the blankets halfway over
       my head,
shiver three times waiting for my heart to keep me warm.

HANDFUL OF INSOMNIA

Only a handful of people
      have given me sleepless nights.

I can count them: son, spouses, Grammy,
      daughter, Dad, and pastor.

And now one client comes with problems
      that feel weighty to hold.

I know I am not to own someone else's troubles;
      however, compassion fatigue is real.

This client survived the holocaust, watched his
      family be killed.

He himself endured experiments, showed me
      where they cut his thumb off.

Unable to trust anyone, he
      eventually learned to trust me.

Such severe PTSD. Once he asked me: "What do
      I do with all of this?"

I responded with: "Write a book," which he
      later did before dying:

Silent Screams Of A Survivor.

TERMINATION

When I bury my face
in your words
it is like course tissue
for my tears.

There are so many places
on and in this body
of bruised veins,
scars for tattoos.

LOA is a polite term
bosses use instead of
"You are no one."
"You are out of here."

Many have pondered secrets
in their wounded hearts.
So few know the proper words
to connect pain to pain.

It's a small town.
I've tried to be no one,
to sit alone in a room
with only a lamp, computer, TV.

Just the computer calls me.
Only what I barely know
can, will and has typed a rug
of mirages under my feet.

A platform without a foundation
yet visible enough for someone

to yank their chain of command.
I cannot stand, but fall to my knees.

That night, drifting off to sleep,
I remember you asking
during your first session:
"Do you like your job?"

This is my answer:
"I love my job. I love it
enough to give you my best,
to go out on a limb I knew
was half-broken."

CAREER CHALLENGE

> "I am always running into
> peoples' unconscious."
> - Marilyn Monroe

It's Wednesday, 4 p.m.
You shuffle in, each week,
holding hands with someone new,
not eager to be here for your court-
ordered counseling. You slouch in
the chair. I pick up clipboard and pen
to hear the same old theme.

In my head I scream—*Where,*
under your pierced tongue, baggy
low-cut pants, knuckles with "love"
"hate," your scraggly chin covered
goatee and tattooed shaven head
do you want to work on your
treatment goals?

Glancing at my client's newfound
sidekick I wonder how she—with
her hip-high vinyl black boots, black
ankle- length sheer coat, purple-pink hair,
pierced tongue and long lacquered nails,
tapping the arm of the lounge chair—
will be of much help to him.

I bite my tongue but want to ask:
when was the last time either of you
listened to a symphony orchestra, or a
decent comedy show, or PG-13 movie or
sat in any kind of church pew and knew any
of the words to a prayer. How many times
have you delayed touching when you felt lust?

New at this career, I
know I am not to judge.
But, dear client, have you considered reading her
heart wrenching poems or notes in the middle
of the night with a flashlight? Or staring up into
the sky and wondering which star belongs to your
true love?

Please tell me, have you ever wondered,
slumped in this office, about the tears
that have rolled down the inside
of my rib cage cradling a heart
that rarely sleeps?

As you swagger out of my office, shoelaces
dangling behind, I ask myself—Are you lost
or is it her, or is it him, or is it me?

AFTER WORKING 8-5

 Give me a pasture
with butterflies and deer—
where I will lay
my head down,
feel the freedom
of my long lost
inner child, who
will take her shoes off,
run through the field
of dreams lingering
from those who have
not yet arrived
in their body.

Give me a plot
of virgin land
with no bones beneath it.

Show me a blue sky
with a summer breeze,
a safe place to exercise
long-forgotten images of
hope, bare feet,
and wings.

BLOWING WORDS

I've got to stop
hanging my hat
on your words—
I'm becoming headless,
nearly helpless waiting
for a morsel, a crumb.

You are no more
to me than a sack
of bones sitting
in my chair, blowing
words toward me,
paying me for my time.

Yet, suddenly, time is all
I have to give you.

You are bringing out of me
all I have only nibbled at.

Sit at my table. Eat at my buffet.
Tell me all about her flaws—
morning, noon and night
'til death do you part
on your next journey.

And I already know
I will miss you more
than the words
you blew my way.

BABE WITH WINGS

For Amber

When you were two
you hated the color orange—
the one color your mother
usually wore, the last shape
you would put into
your plastic shape-o-ball.

You loved birds—
your mother's least
favorite pet,
and boys and men—
the exact opposite gender
of *her.*

You were so much, you
at a young age in a tiny body
knowing how to survive
before its time of knowing
a community of together,
where most chickens refuse
to fly, and caterpillars dream
of sprouting wings at the moment
of their first sunrise- before hope
is shattered by pillars of control
in cities large and small, in
your own neighborhood, under
the roof of your own mother's house.

Gather up scarves of silk
in multi hues of orange and fly,
little one, fly like one
who cannot see the invisible roofs
the pillars think they are
holding up.

CHISELING THE MIRAGE

"Freedom is just another word for nothing
left to lose."
                              - Janis Joplin

Children learn young how to
pirouette in pink tights, kick
balls balanced on one foot.

Better to stand in one room
twirling, twisting, chiseling,
their cortex and feet
letting the air thin their plump
bodies, defeather the hope
caged deep in their ribs,
before walking
neighborhood streets.

For it is there where we lose
our teeth, toys, games,
labeled with names not
mentioned at the tables where
we feast to sustain ourselves.

Rested and grown, I have
watched people slip
fall on thin ice, crash
new cars, be thrown out
of bars, marriages, jobs.

Jailed, divorced, fired,
wired with the anger of their
plumpness they could have
spun off— if only they had known.

Still, oblivious, people are
evicted, disowned, excommunicated,
rejected from universities, sororities,
fraternities, mortgage brokers
and social clubs.

Potential employers will turn you
away for someone younger who
they will then fire for someone
younger still. Perhaps
someone wearing pink tights
who can kick a mean ball.

Your doctor, dentist, psychologist,
priest will have little time for you,
now that there are so many competing
for services to cope with all
the scraping, chiseling of their bones.

Your limbs are bleeding, stones
between your toes.
Don't doze until you scavenge
one more morsel of bread,
breathe deep, bend down.

Take off those tight shoes.
Flip, float or fly inward
to your soul, who
always knows which
direction to go.

ONE'S LIFE IS A MESSAGE

You can celebrate life
become one with it,
jump around or float.

You can dance in circles
believing it's with yourself
when it is twirling
in opposite directions.

You can kill yourself
living life hard, or
you can stand in
one spot and breathe.

You can breathe slowly, or
as if gasping for air
to keep twirling and swirling.

You can breathe standing up,
as if waiting for a marathon, or
sitting down as if
crawling into bed.

I can't tell you how
to live your life
any more than you can
ignore mine.

IV. Healing

Within you there is a stillness and a sanctuary to which you can retreat at times.

—Herman Hesse

COVID NO. 3

It's a fact. I am
much older now.
Blood pulsates through
my veins more slowly.

I am more cautious.
I vaccinate and vaccinate,
booster, cleanse, sanitize
and mask up.

I keep thinking I should
slow down at my age;
yet going, giving, doing and planning
all keep me propelled forward.

So now I sit here
as this sickly virus
runs through the veins
of my life until God heals me.

DEAR KARMA

Dear Karma, you never leave me,
embracing me gently, but oh too long,
surpassing anniversaries and filling
every rock song. How long before you go back
to being an eastern philosophy
and I a simple western poem?

All ropes frazzle somewhere.
All hemp burns sometime.
Undo the knots and neck yourself into a noose.

You woo me knowing well where
my Prince Charming hides. But my lips
you pucker for putting out
birthday candles, sealing thank you notes.

What is a party without kissing?
If he awakens not to me then to whom?
And if not now, when?

Karma, you are a jealous lover
because you know you cannot keep me.
You are a silly cook
because you think the pot
must always brew.
Yet it's not you who nourishes me.
You are only the cook.
He is the food.

NOSTALGIA

Live in the moment they say,
it's mentally healthier.
So, I swear off nostalgia every day.

Then my inner child throws a temper tantrum:
"Where is my rope swing with the wooden seat hanging
from the old oak tree?
The old red flyer sled and hills now leveled
for roads and houses in subdivisions?
Parents who let me climb trees until dark,
let me catch lightening bugs and put them in glass jars
on my nightstand until morning?
Where are the ropes hanging from trees to swing
across creeks where I swam?
Where is my big tractor tire sand box
and my old metal dump-trucks?"

"Where are my hula hoop, jacks, baby doll,
bazooka bubble gum
and TV's *Captain Kangaroo*?
Especially, where is the old wooden barn with the hay loft
where we'd play hide-and-go-seek?"

Giving my inner child a lollipop,
I start reminiscing about college, marriage, raising my
children, my counseling career...so many
memories of mentors, friends, family, fun
times and spiritual highs and lows—little hills
of nostalgia that keep me longing
to wander over and over again.

HOME

He, she, it lives
in Huron. I know it,
as certain as the air
that goes in and out
my nostrils.
In this town,
the one I was sent to,
yet eager to run out of.
The same town you came
to me in January 1973,
in a college classroom.

I still marvel at how
you embrace me—
just as I am—
immobile muscles,
gray hair, wrinkles
tear-stained cheeks.

How could I ever love
another, when
you have silently loved
me all
the days of this life
before what I can
even remember?

I keep moving
thither and outward.
But you still stand still in
one spot and hug me
with arms long and strong
enough to hold up a village.

FATHERS ARE GOOD AUDIENCES

I have watched your eyes dance
as your daughter did ballet.
Seated in the wings,
Standing by the rear door,
I witnessed a solo, duet, trio, symphony all
 on the rug of your living room floor.
And I ended up singing
as she danced through her dreams,
and it seems the sparkle in her eyes
was all the music we needed
for the performance to grow.

FISHERMEN

A man knows when
he has a good bite.
He pulls and tugs,
winds in the line,
uses new lines
and tries again.

When Jesus said, "I will
make you fishers of men,"
some thought "women"
and ran off eagerly
to find bait.

Two thousand years and caution
has taught the female
to avoid lines
and little worms dangling
just below them.

FROM BED TO MOON

You have come out of curiosity,
your parents' pleasure.

A bed—a launching pad
to the moon if you let it.

Let it.
Let the stars guide you
from the pulp to the pillow
so you might lie down
to rest, not breed.
Though breeding will always be
part of the process.
Rest in it.

A church is a church but a bed is
a myriad of steeples pivoting off
one another, upward, seesawing
upward into the sky.

A falling star is nothing
but excitement trailing off
to rest.

SISTER

'O sister, such an engineer
of tall buildings—corporations,
hospitals, sports centers, many
places all over the country.

Even in statue you tower
over me. I look up to you.

Your left-brain skills on a scale always
 out balance my right-brain skills.

You leap over your own buildings,
venture to England, Scotland, Thailand,
Canada, Ireland, Nova Scotia, Alaska
and the U.S.A.

You love building campfires in your back
yard, camping in Maine, Kelly's Island,
the U.P.—building buildings, burning sticks.

Your technical support for this book is
an ember in my heart; and now, retired,
you're writing a novel, doing social work
as a guardian ad litem.

You are a super mother and grandmother as you
travel between Ohio and Texas.

I would paint your legacy now
before your eyes close.
Whispering into your ears:
"I love my sister!"

NO THANK YOU

There is more
than a dead man
walking. There is
an invisible being
yelling whispers into
my ear. Listen.

Don't you feel
the rumblings of the
earth shaking, following
the cries of those who
crossed over too quickly,
unready for the transition?

Limbo is a place in our souls
where we work through
loose ends. Friends are not
something you want to make there.

If I listen too long,
or write a line, they might
assume I am forming a
relationship.

I tell them
I am content to be
here
now
alone,
thank you.

NAMASTE

Melodies in my head—
love poems to you.
No more or less than
love poems in my head
to music.

Swoon with me.
Fly and dip like
a free-falling bird
heading to paradise.

Let the sky, sun
stars, clouds be
notes to our harmony.

No more dusk or dawn,
tears or smiles
for all to read.

Only you and I,
egoless amongst
and within
all creation.

IDLE HANDS CLAPPING

Waiting in the darkness
for the movement
of others to awaken
is a slow dance.

I've had my chance
to tango all day long.

Sometimes an intermission——
taking a so-called "breather"
can lead to the question:
why am I breathing at all?

There was a last call
but I missed it.

Was it on purpose
since I could no longer
discern the dancers
from the music?

The drama is complete
as soon as acknowledged.

It's impossible to close your eyes
when enlightened,
yet difficult to applaud
what seems never ending.

JIM DAY

"Stop looking for a partner. Focus on your goals
and rebuilding your life. The right person will
eventually find their way to you."
- Khalil Habib

Waking up, I wait,
listening for his car
to start
as he drives to work.

Then I realize—
It's Sunday.

I smell
his fiesta eggs wafting
up the stairs.

I rush down
to add the smell
of coffee.

We watch
Sunday Morning
with Jane Pauley.

Feed the birds,
dress to run errands,
take a nap.

Sunday—a day
of rest.
And the rest is
undisclosed.

STILL UNKNOWN

Twenty-five years ago we wed.
Yet, you say I don't know you.

Four years ago I went
to Phoenix to visit a friend,
bought a sterling silver ring
with rose quartz chips on one side.
I have worn it solely on
my left ring finger
where you've never looked.

And I wonder...
when will you discover
the woman you married
all those years ago, who
went to the middle
of the desert,
and renewed her vows
with herself?

RETROSPECT

"Hope' is the thing with feathers-
That perches in the soul—
And sings the tune without the words—
And never stops—at all—"

— Emily Dickinson

When I knew you
were fading,
I painted rainbows
in my heart.

My skin became softer
with longing.
I knew you back then.
I'm still with you now.

I'm not sure
how time passed
so quickly between
the two of us.

You've helped me.
You've hurt me.
You've left me.
You've returned.

There are no words
to explain all
the joy and sorrow
my soul still sorts out.

SUNDAY MORNING

Culinary sounds come
from the kitchen where
he concocts something
as if in a science lab.

She lies on a sofa feeling
the weight of the earth
sink beneath her
vacant thoughts.

Somewhere in the middle,
they will feast on
the leftovers of their lives
and break bread together.

Saints march invisible
through their loose embrace
like lepers counting spots
of unused opportunities.

By dusk they tease
and taunt each other's
differences, like cats
playing with yarn.

And not once will either
speak of their marriage,
their divorce, or all the hours
they continue to spend
with each other waiting
for their new lives to begin.

DRIVING MR. DAISY

> "We are spiritual beings having
> a human experience."
> - Teilhard de Chardin

I married him
because of his humor.

We joked about
me

driving Mr. Daisy
here and there—everywhere

except to his job.
He drove there

to get health insurance
to support him and me.

Said he'd keep going
'til he died in the saddle.

The rides got bumpy.
Aging brings illness.

"For sickness or health,
for better or worse."

So, we make the best of it,
watching our bodies defect.

Still joking and laughing
as I drive Mr. Daisy.

GRACE

I continue to be
baffled by how you pick,
pursue, permeate the pit
of my core—way down so far,
further than my creative
imagination can take me.

No matter where I turn, leap, fall,
your arms are there to hold me
steady from myself.

Somewhere within my tiny toe,
not yet formed on my still
unfamiliar body, I feel my being
bathed in tears of joy, quiver in
a new love, stand steady in
the star dust of my old self.

Your arms are soft pillows
cradling a selfless head that no longer
bobs or turns, just curls up in your lap
in a peaceful repose; no longer
wondering if concrete or clouds are real.

STILL WATERS

> "He leads me beside still waters;
> He restores my soul."
>> - Psalms 23:2

Bloody but bowed,
humbled and crucified
your rod and staff
have kept me from falling
below my knees.

I have walked beside
still waters,
bubbling brooks
even as raindrops kept
falling on my head.

As you continue
to raise me up
to your blessed breast,
a heart so holy
this worm wiggles toward it.

Slowly the ascent—
an inward spiral
to heaven
to the lit manager
of your dwelling.

It is here I kneel,
with wobbly knees,
hands extended
with my overdue
quivering
and bloody heart.

SANCTUARY

Watching him watch her
I did not see in his eyes
visions of sugar plums
or sweet apple pie.

At what point does
the flesh rule
the mind's eye over
our own free will?

Does a blind man see
God more clearly,
or rather fear stumbling
and losing his life?

Older, with scales on my eyes,
I finally see the years
of darkness where I fled
from Thee.

Tasting your sweetness now,
I grope and grapple
toward a sanctuary
in Thee.

SURRENDER

"Lose your soul in God's love…
I swear there is no other way!"
- Rumi

I've run from you,
        rarely humbled myself
            before you.

O creator of shepherds
        above and below the skies,
            within and behind my eyes,
                deep down in my soul.

Beyond my joy and my hurting,
        doing the helping, the healing.

You wrap me around your shoulders
        when I am too weary to walk.

You are the mother and father of my being.
        I surrender my all to you.

photo by Tiffany Branco

Trenda Geller is a native Midwesterner who has traveled extensively. She graduated from Bowling Green State University (B.A.) and the University of Michigan (M.A.). She has published poetry in anthologies: *Prairie Margins* (1975); *Firelands Arts Review* (1977, 1981); *The Heartlands Today* (2002) and *44839 Poetry from a Zip Code-Volume V* (2022). She is a popular reader at Mr. Smith's Coffeehouse Readings in Sandusky, Ohio.

Trenda is a practicing psychotherapist living with her husband James along Lake Erie's shores in Huon, Ohio. She is the parent of two adult children (son deceased).

Trenda states, "Initially I saw poetry as a way to express feelings when adults were too busy to listen. Now poetry has become a way of expressing what I see and listen to in my patients, friends, and family members in our daily life."

OTHER BOOKS BY BIRD DOG PUBLISHING

Shepherds Among Us: Poetic Memoir by Trenda Geller, 110 pgs. $16
Inside the Flow: Poems by Nancy Dunham, 60 pgs. $15
Lost and Found in Alaska by Joel D. Rudinger, 242 pgs. $18
Travis, Texas: A Novel by Gary Harmon 218 pgs. $18
Mingo Town & Memories by Larry Smith, 96 pgs. $15
Road Kill by R. J. Norgard 346 pgs. $18
Trophy Kill by R. J. Norgard, 256 pgs. $16
Symphonia Judaica: Jewish Symphony and Other Poems
by Joel D. Rudinger, 117 pgs. $16
Words Walk: Poems by Ronald M. Ruble, 168 pgs. $16
Homegoing by Michael Olin-Hitt, 180 pgs. $16
A Wonderful Stupid Man: Stories by Allen Frost, 190 pgs. $16
A Poetic Journey, Poems by Robert A. Reynolds, 86 pgs. $16
Dogs and Other Poems by Paul Piper, 80 pgs. $15
The Mermaid Translation by Allen Frost, 140 pgs. $15
Heart Murmurs: Poems by John Vanek, 120 pgs. $15
Home Recordings: Tales and Poems by Allen Frost, $14
A Life in Poems by William C. Wright, $10
Faces and Voices: Tales by Larry Smith, 136 pgs. $14
Second Story Woman: A Memoir of Second Chances
by Carole Calladine, 226 pgs. $15
256 Zones of Gray: Poems by Rob Smith, 80 pgs. $14
Another Life: Collected Poems by Allen Frost, 176 pgs. $14
Winter Apples: Poems by Paul S. Piper, 88 pgs. $14
Lake Effect: Poems by Laura Treacy Bentley, 108 pgs. $14
Depression Days on an Appalachian Farm: Poems
by Robert L. Tener, 80 pgs. $14
120 Charles Street, The Village: Journals & Other Writings 1949-1950
by Holly Beye, 240 pgs. $15

Bird Dog Publishing
http://smithdocs.net

www.ingramcontent.com/pod-product-compliance
Lightning Source LLC
Chambersburg PA
CBHW031143090426
42738CB00008B/1194